Mandala Me Floral
Mandala Coloring Books for
teens and adults

Color and relax coloring perfect creative designs!

by PK Burian

www.pkburian.com
ISBN 13: 978-1533648723
ISBN 10: 1533648727

Introduction

Enter the world of creativity with Mandala Me A Floral Coloring Book. Inside you'll find 30 beautiful mandalas for fun patterning, shading, and coloring. Each detailed mandala will spark your imagination and unleash your artist inside. Printed on high-quality paper, this coloring book for teens and adults is perfect for coloring with markers, colored pencils, or gel pens. Designed to eliminate bleed-through, each page may be removed and displayed.

For more Mandala Me Coloring Books look for:

Mandala Me Beautiful

Mandala Me Animals

Mandala Me Paisley

Mandala Me Paisley Pretty

Mandala Me Love

Mandala Me Hearts

Mandala Me A Holiday

Mandala Me Floral

And for kids:

Animals of the Forest

Bears, Bears, Bears Coloring Book

Bears, Bears, Bears Activity Book

Birds of a Feather

Butterflies Everywhere

Happy Farm Animals

My Favorite Pet

More coming soon!

Proof

Made in the USA
Charleston, SC
07 March 2017